WILD *about* GAME BIRDS

Stoeger Publishing
Great Outdoor Books Since 1925

STOEGER PUBLISHING COMPANY
is a division of Benelli U.S.A.

Benelli U.S.A.
Vice President and General Manager: Stephen Otway
Director of Brand Marketing and Communications:
  Stephen McKelvain
Vice President of Sales/Strategic Marketing:
  Jack Muety

Stoeger Publishing Company
President: Jeffrey Reh
Publisher: Jay Langston
Managing Editor: Harris J. Andrews
Art Director: Cynthia T. Richardson
Imaging Specialist: William Graves
Copy Editor: Kate Baird
Publishing Assistant: Christine Lawton

Published by Stoeger Publishing Company
17603 Indian Head HIghway, Suite 200
Accokeek, Maryland 20607

BK6475
ISBN:0-88317-241-0
Library of Congress Control Number: 2002110162

Manufactured in the United States of America

Distributed to the book trade and
to the sporting goods trade by:
Stoeger Industries
17603 Indian Head HIghway, Suite 200
Accokeek, Maryland 20607

Second of six in the *Wild About* cookbooks series.

Printed in Canada

OTHER PUBLICATIONS:
Shooter's Bible 2003 - 94th Edition
   The World's Standard Firearms Reference Book
Gun Trader's Guide - 25th Edition
   Complete, Fully-illustrated Guide to Modern
   Firearms with Current Market Values

Hunting & Shooting
   Hounds of the World
   The Turkey Hunter's Tool Kit: Shooting Savvy
   Complete Book of Whitetail Hunting
   Hunting and Shooting with the Modern Bow
   The Ultimate in Rifle Accuracy
   Advanced Black Powder Hunting
   Labrador Retrievers
   Hunting America's Wild Turkey
   Taxidermy Guide
   Cowboy Action Shooting
   Great Shooters of the World

Collecting Books
   Sporting Collectibles
   The Working Folding Knife
   The Lore of Spices

Firearms
   Antique Guns
   P-38 Automatic Pistol
   The Walther Handgun Story
   Complete Guide to Compact Handguns
   Complete Guide to Service Handguns
   America's Great Gunmakers
   Firearms Disassembly with Exploded Views
   Rifle Guide
   Gunsmithing at Home
   The Book of the Twenty-Two
   Complete Guide to Modern Rifles
   Complete Guide to Classic Rifles
   Legendary Sporting Rifles
   FN Browning Armorer to the World
   Modern Beretta Firearms
   How to Buy & Sell Used Guns
   Heckler & Koch: Armorers of the Free World
   Spanish Handguns

Reloading
   The Handloader's Manual of Cartridge
Conversions
   Modern Sporting Rifles Cartridges
   Complete Reloading Guide

Fishing
   Ultimate Bass Boats
   The Flytier's Companion
   Deceiving Trout
   The Complete Book of Trout Fishing
   The Complete Book of Flyfishing
   Peter Dean's Guide to Fly-Tying
   The Flytier's Manual
   Flytier's Master Class
   Handbook of Fly Tying
   The Fly Fisherman's Entomological Pattern Book
   Fiberglass Rod Making
   To Rise a Trout

Motorcycles & Trucks
   The Legend of Harley-Davidson
   The Legend of the Indian
   Best of Harley-Davidson
   Classic Bikes
   Great Trucks
   4X4 Vehicles

Cooking Game
   Fish & Shellfish Care & Cookery
   Game Cookbook
   Dress 'Em Out
   Wild About Venison

Contents

4   INTRODUCTION

8   QUAIL

24   PHEASANT

44   WILD TURKEY

66   GROUSE

88   CHUKAR

100   HUNGARIAN PARTRIDGE

110   MOURNING DOVE

126   INDEX

Introduction

This book contains delicious recipes that can be prepared with eight different types of wild game birds: quail *(Coturnix coturnix)*, pheasant of the family Phasianidae, wild turkey *(Meleagris gallopavo)*, ruffed grouse *(Bonasa umbellus)*, chukar, also known as the chukar or rock partridge *(Alectoris chukar)*, sharp-tailed grouse *(Pedioecetes phasianellus)*, Hungarian or gray partridge *(Perdix perdix)* and morning dove *(Zenaida macroura)*. You will learn many methods for preparing these game birds that enhance the flavor and maximize the tenderness of the meat. From the very simple to the highly elaborate, from the traditional to the exotic, from everyday meals to special occasions, there's something for every taste.

Game birds are considered poultry, which is a white meat, although the breast meat of game birds is darker in color. This is due to the muscles involved in flight: These birds, unlike their barnyard cousins, spend much time flying, so their muscles require more oxygen and red blood cells. This results in firmer flesh but does not affect the quality. The meat also has a more distinct taste than that of domestic poultry, but is more delicate than that of other kinds of wild game.

The quality of the meat is determined by the type of food the bird eats, the bird's age and the time of year it is bagged.

1. If the bird feeds on buds or bark, the meat will have a "woody" taste; if it feeds mainly on berries, it will be much milder.
2. The older the bird, the less tender the meat. The meat of older birds will be more tender if it is marinated, braised or simmered, or used to make terrines, pâtés or *tourtes*, etc.
3. A bird bagged in early fall will be tastier because it will have been well nourished throughout the spring and summer. Its meat will contain more fat and will therefore be more tender.

Not everyone appreciates the distinct flavor of game birds. It can be toned down by soaking the meat in milk or in a salt solution of 1 tablespoon (15 milliliters) salt to 4 cups (1 liter) water or a vinegar solution of 1 cup (250 milliliters) vinegar to 4 cups (1 liter) water. This procedure, which also tenderizes the meat, should be done one or two days before the meat is cooked. Unlike marinade, however, the liquid is discarded and not used for other purposes.

Game birds must be eviscerated within the hour after they are killed and refrigerated no more than a few hours later. (They will keep for two or three days in the coldest part of the refrigerator.) The meat deteriorates quickly and can spoil if it is not properly handled. That is why it should be cooked as soon as possible.

Some types of wild game birds are traditionally hung for four to 12 days to allow the proteins to break down, but this is becoming less and less popular. This procedure is said to tenderize the meat and allow it to "get high." Today, it is recommended to hang game birds for three to four days at most. A bird that has been badly damaged must not be hung because the meat may begin to decompose.

For longer storage, game birds can be frozen for up to six months. They must be thawed carefully: Thawing in the refrigerator can take two to six days, depending on the size of the bird. The bird can also be thawed in cold water if it is vacuum-packed. To do so safely, the water must be changed every 30 to 40 minutes so that it remains very cold, and the bird must be kept completely submerged. The microwave oven can also be used, but care must be taken not to cook the meat. When using these last two methods, the birds must be cooked as soon as they have thawed. The meat may be refrozen only after it has been cooked, never when it is uncooked.

Cooking methods are described in each of the sections.

It is possible to substitute one type of game bird for another by adjusting cooking times.

The bones can be used to make savory stocks.

White Stock (Bouillon)

Method

1. Rinse the carcasses and giblets well in cold water.

2. Cook the vegetables without colouring. Set aside

3. Place the carcasses and giblets in a large saucepan and cover with cold water. Bring slowly to a boil and then boil for 10 minutes, skimming constantly in order to clarify the stock.

4. Add the vegetables, thyme and bay leaf. Lower the heat and let simmer for 2 to 3 hours. Add water to compensate for evaporation. Strain the stock through a fine sieve or cheesecloth. Allow to cool, then refrigerate and skim off the fat. Freezes well, divided into smaller portions.

Ingredients

2 lb	game bird carcasses	1 kg
1/4 cup	leek	250 ml
1/4 cup	onion	60 ml
1/4 cup	celery	60 ml
1/4 cup	carrots	60 ml
1 tsp	thyme	5 ml
2	bay leaves	2
6	peppercorns	6
	parsley stalks	
1 tbsp	butter	15 ml
6 cups	cold water	1.5 l

Brown Stock (Bouillon)

4 CUPS

Ingredients

2 lb	game bird carcasses	1 kg
3	carrots, cut into pieces	3
2	stalks celery, cut into pieces	2
2	onions, cut into pieces	2
1/4 cup	tomato paste	60 ml
2	cloves garlic	2
6-8	peppercorns	6-8
2	bay leaves	2
2	sprigs fresh thyme **or**	2
1/2 tsp	dried thyme	2 ml
1	sprig fresh parsley **or**	1
1 tsp	dried parsley	5 ml
6 cups	water	1.5 l

Method

1. In an ovenproof dish, brown the carcasses and the vegetables in the oven at 450°F (225°C) for approximately 15 minutes.
2. Add the tomato paste and bake until the entire mixture is nicely browned.
3. Transfer the mixture to a large pot. Add the remaining ingredients and bring to a boil.
4. Simmer over low heat for 1 1/2 hours.
5. Strain. Use the stock for soups and sauces.

Quail

The sudden explosive flight of a covey of quail, flushed by a hunter's dog or by the tread of an unwary rambler, is a memorable experience of rural life over much of North America. Six species of quail – Bobwhite, California, Montezuma, Gambel's, Mountain, and Scaled –inhabit fields, thickets, scrub, and grasslands across the North American continent, from the semi-desert chaparral of the Southwest to the temperate farmland of the East Coast. The most widespread species, the Bobwhite *(Colinus virginianus)*, is larger than its Old World relatives, averaging from 3 1/2 to 10 ounces (100 to 300 grams). The Mountain quail of northern California and the Pacific Northwest is the largest at about 1 pound (0.5 kg).

Quail are social birds which gather in groups known as coveys. Their mottled plumage, various combinations of brown, black, white, and gray, provides excellent camouflage in tall grasses and brush. The California, Gambel's, and Mountain quails are characterized by a tall teardrop-shaped topknot. They are quick runners. When startled they can instantly burst from a rest into full flight for short distances. Quail are non-migratory and feed on a diet of seeds, berries, green shoots, and insects.

Quail have long been prized for their delicate, tasty, and fairly rich meat, especially when harvested in the early fall. The meat is tender and not overly fatty. Quail are not aged or hung prior to cooking and care must be taken to baste the meat to ensure that it remains moist.

Quail makes a delicate dish when prepared with grapes (Quail with Green Grapes), olives (Mediterranean- Style Quail), citrus fruit (Maple-Glazed Quail with Pink Grapefruit) and dried fruit (Quail with Fruit Stuffing and Two-Mustard Sauce). Quail can be:

- roasted (Roast Quail with Bacon and Spinach);
- braised (Braised Quail with Cumin);
- grilled (Grilled Peppercorn Quail);
- stewed (Honeyed Quail).

The average quail dish generally takes about 20 to 25 minutes to cook. A little extra cooking time should be added for stuffed quail, especially if the stuffing contains meat such as sausage or bacon.

Quail with Fruit Stuffing and Two-Mustard Sauce

Ingredients

Stuffing:

1/2 cup	diced dried apricot	125 ml
1/2 cup	diced red pepper	125 ml
1/2 cup	chopped roasted almonds	125 ml
1/2 cup	cubed Havarti cheese	125 ml
1	shallot, chopped	1
1/2 cup	chopped spinach	125 ml
4	large quail **or**	4
8	small quail	8
1/4 cup	melted butter	60 ml

Sauce:

2	shallots, chopped	2
1 tbsp	butter	15 ml
1 cup	white wine	250 ml
2 tsp	old-fashioned Dijon mustard	10 ml
2 tsp	tarragon Dijon mustard	10 ml
1/2 cup	35% whipping cream	125 ml
	salt and freshly ground pepper to taste	

Method

1. Preheat the oven to 400°F (200°C).
2. Combine all the stuffing ingredients. Season to taste.
3. Stuff the quail with the mixture and place them in a buttered ovenproof dish. Brush the quail with butter and cook in the center of the oven for 25 to 30 minutes. Brush the quail a few times with the melted butter that has accumulated in the dish.
4. Meanwhile, sauté the shallots for 2 to 3 minutes in the butter. Deglaze the pan with the wine. Reduce by half.
5. Add the two mustards and the cream, and reduce until thickened. Adjust the seasoning.
6. Serve the quail on a bed of sauce, along with green vegetables and mashed potatoes.

Maple-Glazed Quail
with Pink Grapefruit

Ingredients

2 tbsp	oil	30 ml
1 tbsp	butter	15 ml
4	large quail, cut in half **or**	4
8	small quail, cut in half	8
1	shallot, finely chopped	1
3/4 cup	pink grapefruit juice	180 ml
1/3 cup	maple syrup	80 ml
1 tbsp	flour	15 ml
2 tbsp	butter, at room temperature	30 ml
	salt and freshly ground pepper to taste	

Garnish:

	pink grapefruit slices	
4	sprigs of herbs (rosemary, tarragon, sage or parsley)	4

Method

1. In a skillet, heat the oil and melt the butter over high heat. Sear the quail halves on both sides, season and transfer to another dish. Keep warm.

2. In the same skillet, cook the shallot in the remaining fat.

3. Deglaze with the grapefruit juice and reduce by a quarter.

4. Add the maple syrup and bring to a boil. In the meantime, blend the flour and the butter into a smooth paste and whisk into the boiling liquid. Simmer until thickened.

5. Place the quail halves in the sauce, along with any cooking juices. Continue cooking until they are glazed with the maple syrup-grapefruit juice mixture and no excess liquid remains.

6. Serve two or four quail halves per portion, depending on the size of the pieces. Garnish with the grapefruit slices and a sprig of herb (rosemary, tarragon, sage or parsley).

Quail with Green Grapes

4 SERVINGS

Ingredients

8	small quail **or**	8
4	large quail	4
1 tbsp	oil	15 ml
1 tbsp	butter	15 ml
2	shallots, finely chopped	2
1/2 cup	red wine	125 ml
1 cup	brown poultry stock	250 ml
1 tbsp	flour	15 ml
1 tbsp	butter	15 ml
24	seedless green grapes, halved	24
2 tbsp	chopped fresh chervil	30 ml
	salt and freshly ground pepper to taste	

Method

1. Preheat the oven to 350°F (180°C).
2. In a pot, brown the quail in the oil and butter over medium heat. Remove the quail and reserve.
3. Add the shallots to the pot and cook for 1 to 2 minutes.
4. Deglaze with the red wine and reduce the liquid by half.
5. Stir in the stock, bring to a boil and simmer for 2 minutes.
6. In the meantime, combine the flour and butter to make a smooth paste. Whisk into the stock. Simmer for 1 to 2 minutes and season.
7. Return the quail to the sauce and bake in the oven for 25 to 30 minutes, depending on size.
8. Add the grapes and chervil. Adjust the seasoning. Serve with your favorite side dishes.

Mediterranean-Style Quail

4 SERVINGS

Ingredients

2 tbsp	olive oil	30 ml
8	small quail **or**	8
4	large quail	4
1	red onion, sliced	1
1/2 lb	mushrooms, halved	225 g
1	yellow summer squash, cut into chunks	1
2	cloves garlic, chopped	2
	juice of 1 lemon	
2	tomatoes, diced	2
1/2 cup	sliced black olives	125 ml
1-2	sprigs fresh rosemary	1-2
	salt and freshly ground pepper to taste	

Method

1. Preheat the oven to 375°F (190°C).
2. In a large skillet, heat the oil and brown the quail on all sides. Place in an ovenproof dish.
3. In the same skillet, saute the onion, mushrooms, squash and garlic and add to the quail.
4. Sprinkle with the lemon juice and stir in the tomatoes, olives and rosemary. Season.
5. Cover and bake in the oven for 20 to 25 minutes.
6. Remove the rosemary and adjust the seasoning. Serve the quail over the vegetable mixture.

Grilled Peppercorn Quail

Ingredients

Marinade:

1	clove garlic, crushed	1
1/2 cup	orange juice	125 ml
3 tbsp	oil	45 ml
20	peppercorns	20
2	green onions, sliced	2
4	large quail, cut in half **or**	4
8	small quail, cut in half	8

Method

1. Combine all the marinade ingredients.
2. Pour the marinade into a large, shallow dish.
3. Place the quail halves in the marinade and let stand for 30 minutes to 6 hours.
4. Place a square of parchment on top of a sheet of aluminum foil.
5. Place two or four quail halves (depending on the size of the quail) on each parchment square. Fold up the a aluminum foil to make a packet. Drizzle with the marinade, close the packets and seal tightly.
6. Cook over a hot grill or in the oven at 375°F (190°C) for 25 to 30 minutes.

Roast Quail with Bacon and Spinach

4 SERVINGS

Ingredients

4	large quail **or**	4
8	small quail	8
	salt and freshly ground pepper to taste	
1	bunch spinach (large leaves), washed and drained	1
8	slices bacon	8

Method

1. Preheat the oven to 400°F (200°C).
2. Rinse the quail and sprinkle with salt and pepper.
3. Cover each quail with spinach leaves and bacon, and tie with string.
4. Bake in the oven for 20 to 25 minutes.
5. Remove the string and serve whole or halved.

Braised Quail with Cumin

Ingredients

2 tbsp	oil	**30 ml**
1 tbsp	butter	**15 ml**
4	large quail, cut in half **or**	**4**
8	small quail, cut in half	**8**
1	onion, chopped	**1**
1-2	cloves garlic, chopped	**1-2**
1	red pepper, diced	**1**
2	stalks celery, sliced	**2**
2 cups	cooked beans (red or white kidney beans, *flageolets*, etc.)	**500 ml**
3/4 cup	miniature corn, cut into chunks	**180 ml**
1 1/2 cups	poultry stock	**375 ml**
1	bay leaf	**1**
1/2-1 tsp	ground cumin	**2-5 ml**
	salt and freshly ground pepper to taste	

Method

1. In a large pot, heat the oil and melt the butter. Sear the quail. Remove from the pot and reserve.
2. Cook the onion, garlic, red pepper and celery in the remaining fat.
3. Add the beans and corn and cook for 2 minutes.
4. Add the stock and bring to a boil.
5. Add the quail, bay leaf and cumin and season with salt and pepper. Cover and simmer for 15 to 20 minutes.
6. Serve two or four (depending on size of quail) quail halves per portion on a bed of vegetables and beans. Spoon a little stock over the quail.

Quail with Red Cabbage and Basil

Ingredients

4	large quail **or**	4
8	small quail	8
2 tbsp	oil	30 ml
2 tbsp	butter	30 ml
1 (1 lb)	red cabbage, thinly sliced	1 (450 g)
1	onion, sliced	1
2	cloves garlic, chopped	2
1/3 cup	balsamic vinegar	80 ml
1/2 cup	red wine	125 ml
1/2 cup	poultry stock	125 ml
	salt and freshly ground pepper to taste	
2 tbsp	chopped fresh basil	30 ml

Method

1. Preheat the oven to 375°F (190°C).
2. In a large pot, heat the oil and melt the butter over high heat.
3. Sear the quail in the very hot mixture of oil and butter. Reserve.
4. Cook the red cabbage, onion and garlic in the remaining fat.
5. Deglaze with the vinegar and wine, and reduce by half.
6. Add the stock, season and bring to a boil. Add the basil.
7. Place the red cabbage mixture in a casserole and add the quail. Cover and bake in the oven for about 20 minutes. Adjust the seasoning.
8. Serve the quail on a bed of red cabbage, garnished with the fresh basil.

Honeyed Quail

Ingredients

1 tbsp	oil	15 ml
1 tbsp	butter	15 ml
4	large quail **or**	4
8	small quail	8
1	clove garlic, crushed	1
1	shallot, finely chopped	1
1 tbsp	flour	15 ml
3/4 cup	dry white wine	180 ml
1/4 cup	honey	60 ml
1 tbsp	Dijon mustard	15 ml
	salt and freshly ground pepper to taste	

Method

1. In a skillet, heat the oil and melt the butter over medium heat and brown the quail on all sides. Reserve.
2. In the same skillet, cook the garlic and shallot in the remaining fat over medium heat.
3. Sprinkle with the flour and deglaze with the white wine.
4. Add the honey and mustard. Bring to a boil and then lower the heat and simmer for 5 minutes.
5. Return the quail to the skillet, season to taste. Cover and cook for 15 to 20 minutes over low heat.
6. Serve the quail with puréed winter squash.

Quail with Wild Mushrooms

If wild mushrooms are unavailable, use one of the many varieties of fresh cultivated mushrooms available: oyster mushrooms, shiitakes, portobellos, etc. Dried mushrooms also work well once they have been rehydrated.

Ingredients

3 tbsp	butter	45 ml
3	shallots, finely chopped	3
4 cups	mixed mushrooms, sliced	1 l
1/4 cup	chopped fresh parsley	60 ml
4	large quail **or**	4
8	small quail	8
1/2 cup	white wine	125 ml
	salt and freshly ground pepper to taste	

Method

1. Preheat the oven to 350°F (180°C).
2. In a skillet, sauté the shallots and mushrooms in the butter over medium heat. Season and transfer to a casserole or other ovenproof dish.
3. Sprinkle the parsley over the mushrooms.
4. In the same skillet, brown the quail on all sides in the remaining butter. Place on the mushrooms.
5. Deglaze the skillet with the white wine and pour the mixture over the quail. Cover and bake in the oven for 20 to 30 minutes.
6. Serve the quail on a bed of mushrooms.

Pheasant

A native of Asia, the male Ring-necked Pheasant *(Phasianus colchicus)* has long been prized by hunters for its size and magnificent plumage. Brought by the Romans to Western Europe, attempts were made to introduce pheasants as domestic and game birds in North America as early as the 1730s. It was not until 1881, however, that the first Ring-necks were successfully established as wild birds in Oregon's Willamette Valley. Since then the pheasant has been established across much of the northern and central United States and central Canada.

Pheasants are medium-sized birds, with males averaging 2 1/2 to 3 pounds and females around 2 pounds. Pheasants prefer areas where agricultural crops and other vegetation provide food and cover. Cultivated and fallow farm fields interspersed with patches of brush, roadside hedgerows, and woodlots generally afford the best habitat for Ring-necks. In the wild pheasants feed on weed seeds and plant shoots and can often be found gleaning waste grains in harvested fields in the fall.

In addition to wild birds, dressed and frozen farm-raised Ring-necks are available commercially. Generally, farm-raised pheasants do not have the same flavor as wild birds. Pheasant meat tends to be dry, even in young birds, and is usually roasted with a moist stuffing. It is very important to bard – to wrap the bird in fat meat, such as bacon or salt pork – or baste it to prevent the meat from drying out during the cooking process. The meat of older birds is less tender and better prepared by simmering or stewing. Older birds can be cooked in terrines (pottery casseroles) or pâtés (baked in a pastry crust). The female pheasant is plumper and more tender. While roasting or broiling pheasant frequent basting is essential and cooking time must be monitored carefully, since the bird dries out quickly when it is overcooked. Pheasant can be:

- roasted (Roast Pheasant with Hazelnut Butter);
- braised (Caribbean-Style Pheasant);
- grilled (Grilled Pheasant with Coriander);
- simmered (Pheasant in Tarragon Orange Cream).

Pheasant is traditionally prepared with wine or spirits and older birds should be hung for two or three days in a cool dry place (30-40°F), provided they have not been badly damaged.

Sesame Pheasant

Ingredients

Marinade:

1/4 cup	oil	60 ml
1-2	cloves garlic	1-2
2 tbsp	rice vinegar	30 ml
2-3 tbsp	toasted sesame oil	30-45 ml
2 tbsp	soy sauce	30 ml
	pinch of Chinese five-spice powder	
1-2 tbsp	honey	15-30 ml
1	pheasant, cut into 10 pieces	1
2-3 tbsp	oyster sauce	30-45 ml
2-3 tbsp	toasted sesame seeds	30-45 ml

Method

1. Combine all the marinade ingredients and marinate the pheasant pieces for 30 minutes to 6 hours.

2. Remove the pheasant pieces and reserve the marinade.

3. Brown the pheasant pieces in a nonstick skillet or wok over high heat.

4. Add the marinade, cover and cook over medium heat until the pheasant is done.

5. Stir in the oyster sauce and sesame seeds. Bring to a boil and reduce by half.

6. Serve hot with rice and sautéed vegetables.

Pheasant in Tarragon Orange Cream

Ingredients

1	whole pheasant, skin removed	1
6 cups	water	1.5 l
1	onion, chopped	1
1	carrot, diced	1
1	stalk celery, diced	1
1	bouquet garni	1
1/4 cup	butter, at room temperature	60 ml
1/4 cup	flour	60 ml
1/2 cup	35% whipping cream	125 ml
2 tbsp	chopped fresh tarragon	30 ml
	zest of 1 orange	
	salt and freshly ground pepper to taste	

Method

1. In a saucepan, combine the first 6 ingredients. Bring to a boil and simmer for 1 hour over low heat until the pheasant is done. Remove the meat and strain the stock.

2. Combine the butter and flour to make a smooth paste.

3. Thicken the stock with the butter-flour mixture until it reaches the desired consistency.

4. Debone the pheasant and dice the meat. Return the meat to the stock.

5. Stir in the cream, tarragon and orange zest. Season to taste.

6. Serve accompanied with fresh bread.

Pheasant Legs with Mushroom, Apple and Fennel Salad

Ingredients

Mustard Dressing:

1/4 cup	Dijon mustard	60 ml
2/3 cup	cider vinegar	160 ml
1 1/3 cups	oil	330 ml
	salt and freshly ground pepper to taste	

4	pheasant legs	4
1/2 lb	mushroom halves, blanched	225 g
3	red apples, sliced	3
1/2	fennel bulb, thinly sliced	1/2
4	beds of mixed lettuce or mesclun	4

Method

1. Prepare the dressing by combining the mustard and cider vinegar.
2. Gradually whisk in the oil to create an emulsion. Add a generous quantity of pepper.
3. Use half the dressing to marinate the pheasant legs for a minimum of 30 minutes. Salt the remaining dressing.
4. In the meantime, combine the blanched mushrooms, sliced apples and sliced fennel. Add the remaining dressing and reserve.
5. Remove the pheasant legs from the marinade and drain well. Grill on a preheated grill at medium heat or broil in the oven at 375°F (190°C) for about 30 minutes.
6. Serve the pheasant legs on a bed of lettuce, with the mushroom, apple and fennel salad.

Caribbean-Style Pheasant

4 SERVINGS

Coconut flakes may be used instead of grated coconut. For a creamier sauce, thicken the cooking juices with butter and flour.

Ingredients

1	pheasant, cut into quarters	**1**
	juice of 3 limes	
2-3 tbsp	oil	**30-45 ml**
2	cloves garlic, crushed	**2**
1/4 cup	sliced green onion	**60 ml**
1 can (19 oz)	pineapple slices	**1 can (540 ml)**
2 tbsp	unsweetened grated coconut	**30 ml**
	pinch of cayenne pepper	
	salt to taste	

Method

1. Pour the lime juice over the pheasant pieces. Let stand in a cool place for 30 minutes.
2. Preheat the oven to 400°F (200°C).
3. In a skillet, heat half the oil and cook the garlic and green onion over low heat, without browning them. Transfer to a casserole.
4. Add the remaining oil and brown the pheasant pieces over high heat, 3 to 4 minutes per side. Transfer to the casserole and reserve.
5. Drain the pineapple and reserve the juice. Pour the juice over the pheasant pieces. Cover and place in the oven for 30 to 45 minutes.
6. Meanwhile, in the same skillet, brown the pineapple slices with the coconut and cayenne pepper.
7. Serve the pheasant pieces with slices of pineapple and the cooking juices.

Pheasant with Lemon Grass

4 SERVINGS

Ingredients

1	pheasant, cut into 10 pieces	1
4	stalks lemon grass, sliced	4
4	green onions, sliced	4
1	clove garlic, crushed	1
2 tsp	salt	10 ml
1/4 tsp	freshly ground pepper	1 ml
2 tbsp	oil	30 ml
1/2 tsp	crushed chili pepper **or**	2 ml
1	fresh chili pepper, chopped	1
2 tsp	sugar	10 ml
1 cup	poultry stock	250 ml
1	red pepper, cut into strips	1
2 tbsp	fish sauce (nuoc nam) (may be obtained in Asian food markets)	30 ml
Garnish:		
1/4 cup	chopped roasted peanuts	60 ml
1/4 cup	chopped fresh coriander	60 ml

Method

1. In a bowl, combine the pheasant pieces, lemon grass, green onions, garlic, salt and pepper. Refrigerate for 30 minutes.

2. In a large saucepan, heat the oil and sauté the pheasant pieces over high heat, 3 minutes per side.

3. Add the chili pepper, sugar, stock and red pepper strips. Simmer until the pheasant pieces are well done (about 30 to 40 minutes). Stir in the fish sauce at the last minute.

4. Garnish with the peanuts and coriander and serve with crispy noodles.

Pheasant with Dried Tomatoes

4 SERVINGS

To rehydrate dried tomatoes, soak in hot water for 10 to 15 minutes and drain well before using. Dried tomatoes in oil may also be used.

Ingredients

Dried Tomato Pesto:

1 cup	dried tomatoes, rehydrated	250 ml
2	cloves garlic	2
2-3 tbsp	roasted pine nuts	30-45 ml
1/2 cup	olive oil	125 ml
2 tbsp	grated Parmesan	30 ml
	salt and freshly ground pepper to taste	

1/4 cup	oil	60 ml
1	pheasant, cut into 10 pieces	1
1	zucchini, sliced	1
1	carrot, sliced	1
1	onion, sliced	1
1	stalk celery, sliced	1
1	pepper (green, red or yellow), sliced	1

Method

1. In a food processor, chop the dried tomatoes with the garlic and pine nuts.
2. Gradually pour in the olive oil.
3. Add the Parmesan and season generously. Reserve.
4. Preheat the oven to 375°F (190°C).
5. In a skillet, heat the oil and brown the pheasant pieces. Place in a casserole.
6. Sauté the vegetables in the skillet and add to the pheasant pieces.
7. Spread the tomato pesto over the pheasant pieces and vegetables. Cover and bake in the center of the oven for about 30 minutes, or until the meat separates easily from the bone.
8. Serve over pasta.

Grilled Pheasant
with Peach Salsa

Ingredients

Marinade:

1/3 cup	lemon juice	80 ml
1/4 cup	oil	60 ml
1	clove garlic, crushed	1
1/2 tsp	salt	2 ml
1/4 tsp	freshly ground pepper	1 ml
1/2 tsp	fresh thyme	2 ml
1	pheasant, cut into quarters	1

Peach Salsa:

4	peaches, peeled and finely diced (papaya **or** pineapple may be substituted)	4
1/4 cup	chopped red onion	60 ml
1/4 cup	chopped red pepper	60 ml
1 tbsp	chopped fresh mint	15 ml
2 tbsp	lime juice	30 ml
1 tbsp	rice vinegar	15 ml

Method

1. Vigorously whisk together the lemon juice, oil, garlic, salt, pepper and thyme.

2. Place the pheasant in a deep dish, pour the marinade over them, cover tightly and refrigerate for 2 to 6 hours.

3. Prepare the salsa at least 30 minutes in advance. Combine all the ingredients and refrigerate until ready to serve.

4. Remove the pheasant pieces from the marinade and grill over medium heat for 20 to 30 minutes.

5. Serve with the peach salsa.

Roast Pheasant with Hazelnut Butter

4 SERVINGS

Ingredients

1 cup	salted butter, at room temperature	250 ml
3/4 cup	chopped roasted hazelnuts	180 ml
2 tbsp	chopped fresh parsley	30 ml
2 tsp	freshly ground pepper	10 ml
1	whole pheasant	1
1 cup	poultry stock	250 ml
2 tbsp	flour	30 ml
1/4 cup	cold water	60 ml

Method

1. Preheat the oven to 375°F (190°C).
2. Combine the butter, hazelnuts, parsley and pepper then insert the butter mixture between the skin and the meat, pushing it toward the neck.
3. Smooth out the skin to distribute the butter evenly.
4. Place the pheasant in an ovenproof dish. Add the stock. Roast in the center of the oven for 45 to 60 minutes.
5. Pour the cooking juices into a saucepan and bring to a boil.
6. Combine the flour with the cold water. Gradually stir it into the cooking juices until a smooth, creamy sauce is obtained.
7. Serve the pheasant with the sauce.

Grilled Pheasant with Coriander

4 SERVINGS

Ingredients

1	pheasant, cut in half	1
1 tbsp	vegetable oil	15 ml
1 tbsp	butter	15 ml
1	shallot, chopped	1
1 cup	poultry stock	250 ml
	pinch of saffron	
1 cup	35% whipping cream	250 ml
1/2 cup	chopped fresh coriander	125 ml
	salt and freshly ground pepper to taste	

Method

1. Preheat the barbecue to 350°F (180°C).
2. Brush the pheasant halves with the oil and grill for 20 to 30 minutes, turning once. Season.
3. In the meantime, melt the butter in a saucepan and cook the shallot.
4. Add the stock and saffron, and reduce by a third.
5. Stir in the cream and continue cooking until a smooth, creamy texture is obtained. Adjust the seasoning. Keep warm.
6. Just before serving, add the coriander to the sauce.

Wild Coq au Vin

Ingredients

1/4 lb	lardons (sliced salt pork or bacon)	115 g
2 tbsp	oil	30 ml
1 tbsp	butter	15 ml
	flour seasoned with salt and pepper	
1	pheasant, skin removed, cut into 10 pieces	1
1 1/2 cups	peeled pearl onions	375 ml
2 cups	white mushrooms, quartered	500 ml
1 cup	dry red wine	250 ml
2 cups	poultry stock	500 ml
1	bouquet garni	1
1	clove garlic	1
	salt and freshly ground pepper to taste	
2-3 tbsp	chopped fresh parsley	30-45 ml

Method

1. Blanch the lardons in boiling water. Drain and reserve.
2. In a large saucepan, heat the oil and melt the butter.
3. Dredge the pheasant pieces in flour and brown them in the oil-butter mixture. Reserve.
4. Cook the onions and mushrooms in the remaining fat. Reserve.
5. Deglaze the saucepan with the red wine, reduce by a third and add the stock.
6. Add the bouquet garni and garlic. Season generously with salt and pepper. Bring to a boil.
7. Place the pheasant pieces and the lardon in the liquid. Cover and simmer for 30 to 45 minutes or bake in the oven at 350°F (180°C).
8. Strain the liquid. Remove the bouquet garni and garlic clove. Remove the pheasant pieces.
9. Adjust the seasoning and the consistency of the sauce. Thicken with butter and flour, if necessary.
10. Return the pheasant pieces to the sauce and add the onions and mushrooms. Simmer for 5 to 10 minutes before serving.
11. Sprinkle with the fresh parsley and top with croutons.

Pheasant Stuffed with Leek and Apple

Ingredients

1	whole pheasant	1
2 tbsp	butter	30 ml
2	leeks, white part, sliced	2
2	apples, peeled and diced	2
1/2 cup	cider **or** white vermouth	125 ml
1-2 tbsp	fresh herbs (sage, tarragon, rosemary, etc.)	15-30 ml
1/2 lb	ground chicken or other poultry, uncooked	225 g
1-2 tbsp	melted butter	15-30 ml

Sauce:

1/2 cup	cider **or** white vermouth	125 ml
1 cup	unsweetened apple juice	250 ml
1 tbsp	flour	15 ml
1 tbsp	butter, at room temperature	15 ml
1/2 cup	35% whipping cream	125 ml
	salt and freshly ground pepper to taste	

Method

1. Preheat the oven to 375°F (190°C).
2. Place the pheasant in an ovenproof dish, breast side up.
3. In a skillet, melt the butter and cook the sliced leeks and diced apples.
4. Deglaze with the cider and reduce until nearly dry. Season generously and add the herbs. Let cool.
5. Combine the leek-and-apple mixture with the ground meat to make the stuffing.
6. Fill the cavity of the bird with stuffing, without pressing too hard, and tie the pheasant. Baste the breasts with melted butter.
7. Cook in the center of the oven for about 1 1/2 hours.
8. Prepare the sauce in the skillet used for the leeks and apples. Reduce the cider and apple juice by half.
9. In the meantime, combine the flour and butter into a paste and whisk it into the apple juice and cider reduction until it thickens.
10. Add the cream and seasoning to the sauce. Flavor with herbs, if desired.
11. Place the stuffed pheasant on a serving platter.

Wild Turkey

The largest and most spectacular of the North American game birds, the wild turkey *(Meleagris gallopavo)* is the monarch of the deciduous forests of the eastern and southern United States. By 1900 the wild turkey had been forced to the brink of extinction by over-hunting and destruction of habitat. In the last half of the twentieth century an amazingly successful program of restocking sponsored by local wildlife agencies and organizations of concerned sportsmen, assisted by widespread re-forestation, has restored wild turkey populations across much of its original range.

The wild turkey was an important food source for both Native Americans and Colonial settlers. Several Indian groups fashioned ceremonial cloaks from the iridescent breast feathers of the males. The Aztecs and other Mesoamerican civilizations domesticated the wild turkey and it became a key ingredient in one of Mexico's national dishes, *Guajolote en Mole Plobano* (which also contains chocolate). Early Spanish explorers, observing some similarities between the African guinea fowl – a semi-domestic bird introduced into Europe via Asia Minor – and the North American turkey incorrectly dubbed the latter a "turkey."

Wild turkeys roost in trees at night and forage on the forest floor during the day for mast (acorns, hickory nuts, seeds, etc) and plant shoots. Turkeys gather in flocks – a female and her brood or groups of gobblers – and a dominant tom and hens during mating season. Wild turkeys use an extensive system of calls to maintain social groups and gobblers make elaborate displays for dominance and mating. Turkeys are wary and elusive game birds, with excellent vision and quick reactions, capable of running rapidly on the ground or bursting into swift and powerful flight.

The average male wild turkey weighs perhaps 17 pounds (7.7 kg). Unlike its grossly overweight domestic cousin, the wild turkey has little fat and can be less tender, The meat of the wild female turkey is succulent, while the meat of the male bird is drier and is best prepared in a sauce.

Turkey can be prepared in many different ways:

- roasted (Wild Turkey with Capers);
- grilled (Cajun-Style Wild Turkey);
- stewed (Simmered Wild Turkey with Onions);
- sautéed (Saltimbocca Sauté);
- fried (Crispy Wild Turkey Cutlets with Saffron Sauce).

With careful preparation this game bird has something for every taste, from the classic to the exotic.

Wild Turkey Confit

The duck or goose fat may be replaced by lard, but it will taste milder and will contain more cholesterol.

Ingredients

1 tbsp	coarse salt	**15 ml**
1 tbsp	sugar	**15 ml**
2 tbsp	cracked peppercorns	**30 ml**
2	bay leaves	**2**
1 tsp	dried thyme	**5 ml**
1	clove garlic, sliced	**1**
2	wild turkey legs	**2**
	duck or goose fat (to cover)	

Method

1. Combine the salt, sugar, peppercorns, bay leaves, thyme and garlic. Coat the turkey legs with this mixture. Let stand for 1 1/2 hours.

2. Rinse the turkey legs under running water to remove the salt and drain well between two sheets of paper towel.

3. In an ovenproof dish, melt the fat. Add the turkey legs. Cover and cook at 200°F (100°C) for 3 to 6 hours, until the meat is tender.

4. Serve the turkey legs hot or cold, whole or shredded. The meat can also be used for canapés and other appetizers.

Asian Mushroom Soup

Ingredients

1 tbsp	oil	**15 ml**
1	clove garlic, chopped	**1**
1 tbsp	chopped fresh ginger	**15 ml**
1 cup	shiitake mushrooms, sliced	**250 ml**
1	onion, sliced	**1**
1	stalk celery, sliced	**1**
1	carrot, julienned	**1**
4 cups	poultry stock	**1 l**
1	wild turkey leg, with skin	**1**
2 tbsp	soy sauce	**30 ml**
2 tbsp	tomato paste	**30 ml**
2 tbsp	rice or cider vinegar	**30 ml**
3 tbsp	brown sugar	**45 ml**
1 tbsp	sesame oil	**15 ml**
2 tbsp	cornstarch	**30 ml**
	salt and freshly ground pepper to taste	

Garnish:

chopped fresh coriander

Method

1. In a saucepan, heat the oil and lightly brown the garlic and ginger.

2. Add the mushrooms, onion, celery and carrot and cook for 4 to 5 minutes over low heat. Remove from the saucepan and reserve.

3. Pour in the stock and add the turkey leg. Bring to a boil and simmer for 30 to 40 minutes or until the meat separates from the bone.

4. Remove the meat from the stock. Let cool and remove the bones. In the meantime, combine the soy sauce, tomato paste, vinegar, brown sugar and sesame oil.

5. Add this mixture to the hot stock, along with the meat and vegetables.

6. Thicken with the cornstarch combined with a little water.

7. Season to taste. Ladle into bowls and garnish with the coriander.

Cajun-Style Wild Turkey

Ingredients

Marinade:

2 tbsp	Cajun spice*	30 ml
1/4 cup	oil	60 ml
	juice of 1/2 lime	
2	cloves garlic, chopped	2
	salt and freshly ground pepper to taste	
2 lb	skinned wild turkey pieces	1 kg

Sour Cream with Herbs:

1 cup	sour cream	250 ml
2	green onions, chopped, **or**	2
1/4 cup	chopped chives	60 ml
1 tbsp	chopped fresh coriander	15 ml
1 tbsp	chopped fresh parsley	15 ml
1	clove garlic, chopped	1
	salt and freshly ground pepper to taste	

* Cajun spice: A blend of garlic powder, onion, paprika, chiles, black pepper, mustard and celery, usually available in most grocery stores.

Method

1. In a large bowl, combine the Cajun spice, oil, lime juice, garlic, salt and pepper. Add the turkey pieces and stir to coat well. Marinate for 30 minutes to 6 hours in the refrigerator.

2. Combine the sour cream, onions, herbs, garlic, salt and pepper. Refrigerate.

3. Grill the turkey pieces on a preheated grill for 25 minutes (or more, depending on the size of the pieces) over medium heat, turning often.

4. Serve with the sour cream dip.

Wild Turkey
with Herbes de Provence

Once the cooking juices are added to the mayonnaise, it must be used within two days. Regular homemade mayonnaise keeps for four or five days.

Ingredients

2 lb	skinned wild turkey	**1 kg**
1-2 tsp	olive oil	**5-10 ml**
2-3 tbsp	Herbes de Provence (basil, rosemary, bay leaf, savory and thyme)	**30-45 ml**
	salt and freshly ground pepper to taste	

Homemade Mayonnaise:

1	egg yolk	**1**
1-2 tbsp	Dijon mustard	**15-30 ml**
1/2 cup	vegetable oil	**125 ml**
1 tbsp	wine vinegar **or** lemon juice	**15 ml**

Method

1. Place the wild turkey in an ovenproof dish, cavity side down. Brush with the oil and sprinkle generously with the herbs. Season with salt and pepper.

2. Cook at 375°F (190°C) for about 1 hour. Remove from the oven and let stand on a plate to allow cooking juices to drain.

3. In the meantime, beat the egg yolk with the mustard.

4. Add the oil in a thin stream, whisking constantly.

5. Stir in the vinegar and cooking juices from the turkey and season.

6. Serve hot or cold with the mayonnaise.

Crispy Wild Turkey Cutlets with Saffron Sauce

Ingredients

1/3 cup	flour	80 ml
1	egg, beaten	1
1 cup	plain breadcrumbs	250 ml
1/4 cup	grated Parmesan	60 ml
1 tbsp	chopped fresh parsley	15 ml
	salt and freshly ground pepper to taste	
4	wild turkey cutlets, about 1/2 inch (1 cm) thick, flattened	4
	oil for frying	

Sauce:

1 tbsp	butter	15 ml
1	shallot, chopped	1
1 cup	poultry stock	250 ml
	pinch of saffron	
1 tbsp	cornstarch	15 ml
1/2 cup	thick yogurt	125 ml
	salt and freshly ground pepper to taste	

Method

1. Place the flour in a deep plate, the beaten egg in another plate and the breadcrumbs, Parmesan, parsley, salt and pepper in a third plate.

2. Dredge the turkey pieces, one at a time, in the flour (shake off any excess). Dip them in the egg and then coat them with the breadcrumb mixture.

3. In a saucepan, melt the butter and sauté the shallot. Add the stock. Bring to a boil and add the saffron. Simmer for a few minutes to allow the saffron to steep.

4. In the meantime, heat the oil over medium heat and cook the breaded cutlets for 3 to 4 minutes per side.

5. Combine the cornstarch with the yogurt and season. Whisk into the hot liquid. Simmer until the mixture thickens.

6. Spoon a little sauce onto the plate and place the crispy turkey cutlets on top. Serve with vegetables and egg noodles.

Simmered Wild Turkey
with Onions

Method

1. Preheat the oven to 350°F (180°C).

2. Dredge the turkey pieces in the flour and shake off any excess.

3. In an ovenproof dish, heat the oil and melt the butter. Sauté the turkey pieces.

4. Add the onions and garlic and cook until they are soft and golden (4 to 5 minutes).

5. Deglaze with the wine and stir in the mustard.

6. Add the stock and season to taste. Bring to a boil, cover and place in the oven for 20 to 25 minutes.

7. Add the potatoes, layering the slices so that the surface of the dish is covered and cook for another 10 minutes. Sprinkle with the Gruyère and place in the oven to melt and toast the cheese.

Ingredients

1 1/3 lb	deboned wild turkey pieces	600 g
	flour seasoned with salt and freshly ground pepper	
2 tbsp	oil	30 ml
1 tbsp	butter	15 ml
3	onions, sliced	3
1	clove garlic, chopped	1
1/2 cup	dry white wine	125 ml
1-2 tbsp	Dijon mustard	15-30 ml
3 cups	poultry stock	750 ml
	salt and freshly ground pepper to taste	
2-3	potatoes, thinly sliced	2-3
1 1/2 cups	grated Gruyère	375 ml

Saltimbocca Sauté

Ingredients

3 tbsp	oil	45 ml
1 1/3 lb	deboned wild turkey pieces	600 g
1/2 cup	thinly sliced Spanish onion	125 ml
1-2 tbsp	chopped fresh sage	15-30 ml
4	slices prosciutto, cut into strips	4
1/2 cup	dry white wine	125 ml
2 tbsp	onion chutney **or** onion confit	30 ml
	salt and freshly ground pepper to taste	

Onion Confit:

2 tbsp	butter	30 ml
2	Spanish onions, thinly sliced	2
1/2 cup	white wine	125 ml
1/2 cup	poultry stock	125 ml
1 cup	sugar	250 ml
1	bay leaf	1
1	sprig thyme	1
	salt and freshly ground pepper to taste	

Method

1. In a large skillet, heat the oil and sauté the turkey pieces and the onion.
2. Add the sage and prosciutto. Continue cooking for another 2 to 3 minutes.
3. Deglaze with the white wine and reduce for 1 minute.
4. Add the chutney and season to taste.
5. Serve with a risotto.

Onion Confit

1. In a saucepan, melt the butter and brown the onions over medium heat until soft.
2. Add the white wine and reduce by half.
3. Stir in the stock, sugar, bay leaf and thyme. Cook until the onions have caramelized and almost all the liquid has evaporated.
4. Season to taste.

The onion confit can be stored in the refrigerator in sterilized jars or preserved in sealed jars for longer storage.

Wild Turkey with Capers

Ingredients

2 lb	wild turkey, cut in half	1 kg

Caper Butter:

1	shallot, finely chopped	1
1/2 cup	butter, at room temperature	125 ml
2 tbsp	finely chopped capers	30 ml
1/2 tsp	freshly ground pepper to taste	2 ml

Sauce:

3 tbsp	oil	45 ml
2 tbsp	drained capers	30 ml
1	shallot, chopped	1
1	clove garlic, chopped	1
1/2 cup	white wine	125 ml
1/3 cup	poultry stock	80 ml
1 cup	prepared demi-glace	250 ml
3 tbsp	35% whipping cream	45 ml
1-2 tbsp	lemon juice	15-30 ml
	salt and freshly ground pepper to taste	

Method

1. Preheat the oven to 400°F (200°C).
2. Place the turkey halves in an ovenproof dish, skin side up.
3. Combine all the ingredients for the caper butter and spread the mixture under the skin.
4. Bake in the center of the oven for 40 to 45 minutes. Baste with poultry stock if necessary.
5. In a skillet, heat the oil and fry the capers until they are crisp. Drain on paper towels. Reserve.
6. In the same skillet, sauté the shallot and garlic in the remaining oil. Drain off any excess oil.
7. Deglaze with the wine and stock and reduce by a third.
8. Add the demi-glace and cream. Simmer until the desired consistency is obtained.
9. Stir in the lemon juice and season. Add the capers just before serving. The meat may be served sliced or separated into breasts and legs.

Wild Turkey
with Smoked Gouda Sauce

Ingredients

3 tbsp	old-fashioned Dijon mustard	45 ml
1 tbsp	honey	15 ml
1 1/3 lb	skinned wild turkey breasts, cut into pieces	600 g

Sauce:

2	shallots, finely chopped	2
1 tbsp	butter	15 ml
1/2 cup	white wine	125 ml
1 cup	35% whipping cream	250 ml
1/2 cup	grated smoked Gouda	125 ml
	flour	
	salt and freshly ground pepper to taste	

Method

1. Preheat the grill or the oven to 400°F (200°C).
2. Combine the mustard and honey. Season.
3. Brush the turkey pieces with the mustard mixture.
4. Cook on the grill or in the oven for 7 to 10 minutes per side.
5. In the meantime, make the sauce. Cook the shallots in the butter for 3 to 4 minutes, over low heat.
6. Deglaze with the white wine and reduce by half. Stir in the cream and reduce by half again.
7. Sprinkle the cheese with flour and add it to the sauce, stirring until it has melted completely. Season to taste.
8. Spoon the sauce over the breasts and serve immediately, accompanied by a summer salad.

Sweet-and-Sour Wild Turkey

Ingredients

Coating:

1/4 cup	all-purpose flour	**60 ml**
1 tsp	garlic powder	**5 ml**
1 tsp	paprika	**5 ml**
1 tsp	salt	**5 ml**
1 tsp	freshly ground pepper	**5 ml**
1 tsp	dry mustard	**5 ml**
1/4 tsp	ground sage **or** bay leaf	**1 ml**

2 lb	skinned wild turkey pieces	**1 kg**
1 tbsp	oil	**15 ml**
1 tbsp	butter	**15 ml**
1	onion, finely chopped	**1**
2 cups	apple juice	**500 ml**
1 tbsp	soy sauce	**15 ml**
	juice of 1/2 lemon	
	freshly ground pepper to taste	

Method

1. In a resealable plastic bag, combine all the coating ingredients.
2. Add the turkey pieces and shake well to coat. Shake off any excess coating.
3. In a skillet, heat the oil and melt the butter over medium heat.
4. Brown the turkey pieces on all sides. Reserve.
5. In the same skillet, cook the onion for 2 minutes.
6. Deglaze with the apple juice, add the soy sauce and lemon juice and return the turkey pieces to the skillet. Cook for 30 to 40 minutes over medium heat. Adjust the seasoning.
7. Serve with sautéed vegetables and rice.

Grouse

In the spring, hardwood forest clearings across the uplands of the eastern and upper United States and much of Canada echo with the distinctive drumming of the Ruffed Grouse, the rapid beating of wings that announce the male's territory. In fact the Ruffed Grouse is only one of the seven species of grouse that inhabit North America. These include the Sharp-tailed Grouse, a native of sagebrush and prairie in the Northwestern Plains States, Alaska, and Western Canada, the Blue Grouse, Spruce Grouse, (which inhabits Canada's northern coniferous forests), the Sage Grouse, Greater Prairie-chicken, and Lesser Prairie-chicken. Male grouse are noted for their elaborate courtship display, called the "lek," characterized by extravagant posturing and shows of fanned tail, erect plumage, and, in some species, colorful inflated air sacs.

Male Ruffed and Sharp-tailed Grouse weigh a little more than a pound (500g). The females of both species are smaller. The Ruffed Grouse's dappled and barred plumage ranges in color from pale gray through dull red and dark brown. Colors reflect their habitat: dark-colored grouse tend to live in dark forest regions, and predominantly gray grouse live in lighter brush country. The Sharp-tail is mainly buff colored, well suited to its habitat of aspen-sagebrush and prairie grass.

The Ruffed Grouse *(Bonasa umbellus)* – the Latin word *Bonasa* translates as "good when roasted" – feeds on forest buds, berries, fruits, and seeds, which can on occasion give the meat a "woody" taste. On the other hand, the Sharp-tailed Grouse *(Tympanuchus phasianellus)*, a grassland dweller, feeds on weed seeds, fruit, and insects, which gives it a very flavorful meat. Cooking times depend on age of the bird. Older birds taste better braised or simmered instead of grilled or roasted. Grouse must not be aged, but tenderizing the meat is recommended by soaking it in milk for periods of several hours to two days prior to cooking. Ruffed and Sharp-tailed grouse can be:

- roasted (Roast Ruffed Grouse with Onion Relish,);
- braised (Sharp-Tailed Grouse Stew with Lentils);
- grilled (Grilled Ruffed Grouse with Maple Syrup);
- stewed or simmered (Ruffed Grouse Simmered in Beer and Sunny Casserole).

Grouse is delicious when prepared with savory ingredients: herbs and spices, fresh or dried fruit. It can be cooked in wine or spirits.

Ruffed Grouse in Green Curry Sauce

4 SERVINGS

4 SERVINGS

The green curry paste may be replaced with red or yellow curry paste.

Ingredients

3 1/2 cups	coconut milk	875 ml
2	grouse, skinned, cut into quarters	2
3 tbsp	store-bought green curry paste	45 ml
1	lemon, sliced	1
1 tsp	salt	5 ml
2 tbsp	fish sauce (nuoc nam) (may be obtained in Asian food markets)	30 ml
1/4 cup	chopped fresh coriander	60 ml

Method

1. In a saucepan, bring the coconut milk to a boil. Reduce by a quarter.
2. Add the grouse pieces and cook over medium heat for 15 to 20 minutes.
3. Add the curry paste, lemon slices, salt and fish sauce. Bring to a boil and cook over low heat for 10 to 15 minutes.
4. Serve over rice and garnish with coriander.

Grilled Ruffed Grouse
with Maple Syrup

Ingredients

Marinade:

1/4 cup	maple syrup	**60 ml**
2 tbsp	Dijon mustard	**30 ml**
1/3 cup	water	**80 ml**
1	small onion, chopped	**1**
1 tsp	fresh thyme	**5 ml**
	freshly ground pepper to taste	
2	ruffed grouse, cut in half	**2**
	salt to taste	

Method

1. Combine the marinade ingredients. Season to taste.

2. Coat the grouse halves with the marinade. Refrigerate overnight.

3. Grill on the barbecue over medium–high heat for 10 to 15 minutes per side. Salt the meat after it is cooked.

Game Bird Jambalaya

Ingredients

2 tbsp	oil	30 ml
1 tbsp	butter	15 ml
2	whole ruffed grouse	2
1 cup	diced ham	250 ml
1	spicy sausage, blanched and sliced	1
1	green pepper, finely diced	1
1	onion, chopped	1
2	stalks celery, sliced	2
4	cloves garlic, chopped	4
3 cups	poultry stock, heated	750 ml
1 1/2 cups	diced tomatoes	375 ml
2	bay leaves	2
1 tsp	dried thyme	5 ml
	salt and freshly ground pepper to taste	
	hot pepper sauce **or** cayenne pepper to taste	
1 cup	long-grain rice	250 ml
1 bunch	green onions, chopped	1 bunch

Method

1. Preheat the oven to 350°F (180°C).
2. In a large pot, heat the oil and melt the butter.
3. Brown the grouse on all sides and reserve.
4. In the same pot, cook the ham with the sausage and vegetables.
5. Add the stock and bring to a boil.
6. Add the remaining ingredients except the rice and green onions. Place the grouse in the center of the pot. Cover and bake in the oven for 30 minutes.
7. Stir in the rice and cook for another 20 minutes.
8. Adjust the seasoning and garnish with the chopped green onions.

Chinese-Style Ruffed Grouse

Ingredients

4	ruffed grouse, whole or cut in half	4

Marinade:

3 tbsp	rice vinegar	45 ml
3 tbsp	soy sauce	45 ml
2 tbsp	marmalade	30 ml
1-2 tsp	toasted sesame oil	5-10 ml
2/3 cup	hoisin sauce	160 ml
1	clove garlic, crushed	1
2 tsp	finely chopped fresh ginger	10 ml
3	green onions, thinly sliced	3

Method

1. Place the grouse in a large pot and cover with water. Bring to a boil and simmer for 30 minutes. Drain.

2. Combine all the marinade ingredients and place the grouse in the marinade.

3. In the meantime, preheat the grill or oven to 375°F (190°C).

4. Place the grouse on an oiled grill and cook for 15 to 20 minutes, basting frequently with the remaining marinade, until they are nicely glazed.

5. Serve a half grouse per portion, sprinkle with the green onions and accompany with a salad.

Roast Ruffed Grouse with Onion Relish

The grouse may also be barbecued.

Ingredients

2	red onions, thinly sliced	2
1/4 cup	freshly squeezed lime juice	60 ml
1 tbsp	ground coriander seeds	15 ml
1/2 cup	julienned cucumber	125 ml
4	ruffed grouse, cut in half	4
1 cup	poultry stock	250 ml
	salt and freshly ground pepper to taste	
	sugar to taste	

Method

1. Preheat the oven to 350°F (180°C).

2. In a bowl, combine the onions, lime juice, coriander and cucumber. Cover and refrigerate for at least 30 minutes.

3. Place the grouse on a baking sheet, brush with the poultry stock and cook in the center of the oven for 25 to 30 minutes, basting frequently. Season to taste.

4. Before serving, season the relish and add sugar if it is too sour.

5. Serve a half grouse per portion, accompanied with the relish.

Ruffed Grouse Simmered in Beer

The prunes may be replaced by other kinds of dried fruit (apricots, raisins, etc.) and a milder beer may be used. The beer may also be replaced by wine or 1/4 cup (60 ml) of Armagnac.

Ingredients

1 tbsp	oil	15 ml
1 tbsp	butter	15 ml
1	onion, finely chopped	1
1	stalk celery, finely chopped	1
2	ruffed grouse, cut into quarters	2
2 tbsp	flour	30 ml
1 1/3 cups	strong beer	341 ml
2 cups	brown poultry stock	500 ml
1	sprig fresh thyme **or**	1
1 tsp	dried thyme	5 ml
1	bay leaf	1
12	pitted prunes	12
	salt and freshly ground pepper to taste	

Method

1. In a pot, heat the oil and butter.
2. Cook the onion and celery. Reserve.
3. In the same pot, brown the grouse pieces on all sides. Return the vegetables to the pot.
4. Remove from heat and sprinkle with flour.
5. Add the beer and stir to blend in the flour.
6. Add the remaining ingredients, season and bring to a boil. Simmer for 20 to 35 minutes, or until the meat separates easily from the bone.
7. Adjust the seasoning. Remove the thyme and bay leaf.
8. Serve with vegetables in season.

Roast Sharp-Tailed Grouse
with Strawberry Port Compote

4 SERVINGS

I n g r e d i e n t s

Compote:

1 tbsp	oil	15 ml
1 tbsp	butter	15 ml
1	shallot, chopped	1
2 cups	washed, hulled and sliced strawberries	500 ml
1/2 cup	port	125 ml
1 tbsp	chopped fresh basil	15 ml
2	sharp-tailed grouse	2
2-3 tbsp	port	30-45 ml
	salt and freshly ground pepper to taste	

M e t h o d

1. In a saucepan, heat the oil and melt the butter. Brown the shallot.
2. Add the strawberries and cook for 2 to 3 minutes.
3. Deglaze with the port over high heat and reduce until nearly dry.
4. Add the basil and season to taste. Reserve.
5. Preheat the oven to 375°F (190°C).
6. Place the grouse in an ovenproof dish, breast side up. Truss if necessary.
7. Baste with the port. Salt and pepper generously.
8. Bake for 30 to 40 minutes in the center of the oven.
9. Arrange on a serving platter and serve with the compote.

Sharp-Tailed Grouse Stew
with Lentils

Ingredients

2	sharp-tailed grouse, cut in half	2
2 tbsp	oil	30 ml
4	cloves garlic, chopped	4
1	onion, chopped	1
2	stalks celery, sliced	2
1 cup	rice	250 ml
2/3 cup	lentils	160 ml
6 cups	poultry stock	1.5 L
1/4 cup	tomato paste	60 ml
2	bay leaves	2
1 tsp	dried thyme	5 ml
	salt and freshly ground pepper to taste	

Method

1. In a large pot, brown the grouse halves in the oil.
2. Add the garlic, onion and celery. Cook for 2 to 3 minutes.
3. Add the rice and lentils. Cook for 1 minute, stirring well so that the mixture is evenly coated with oil.
4. Add the stock and tomato paste. Mix well.
5. Stir in the herbs and season generously.
6. Bring to a boil and simmer for 25 minutes, half-covered, over medium heat.
7. Serve with vegetables.

Sunny Casserole

4 TO 6 SERVINGS

Ingredients

	flour seasoned with salt and pepper	
3	sharp-tailed grouse, cut in quarters	3
1/4 cup	oil	60 ml
2	cloves garlic, chopped	2
1	onion, sliced	1
1	hot pepper (optional)	1
2 cups	poultry stock	500 ml
1 cup	mango juice	250 ml
	zest and juice of 1/2 lime	
	salt and freshly ground pepper to taste	

Lime Mayonnaise:

1	egg yolk	1
1 tbsp	Dijon mustard	15 ml
2/3 cup	vegetable oil	160 ml
	zest and juice of 1/2 lime	
	salt and freshly ground pepper to taste	

Method

Casserole

1. Dredge the grouse pieces in flour and shake off any excess.
2. In a large pot, heat the oil over high heat and sear the grouse pieces on all sides.
3. Add the garlic, onion and whole hot pepper, if desired. Cook for 2 to 3 more minutes.
4. Add the stock, mango juice and lime juice and zest. Season.
5. Partially cover the pot and bring to a boil. Simmer for about 45 minutes over medium heat. Remove the hot pepper. Adjust the seasoning and consistency of the sauce as needed.
6. Serve the grouse over rice with the lime mayonnaise.

Lime Mayonnaise

1. In a bowl, combine the egg yolk and the mustard.
2. Gradually whisk in the oil.
3. Stir in the lime juice and zest. Season generously. Keep in a cool place until ready to serve.

Sharp-Tailed Grouse in Pastry Crust

4 SERVINGS

Ingredients

5 cups	all-purpose flour	1.25 l
2 tbsp	coarse salt	30 ml
1 1/2 cups	cold water	375 ml
	juice and zest of 2 lemons	
2 tbsp	finely chopped fresh thyme	30 ml
3 tbsp	finely chopped fresh oregano	45 ml
2	cloves garlic, crushed	2
1/4 cup	oil	60 ml
	salt and freshly ground pepper to taste	
4	sharp-tailed grouse	4

Method

1. Preheat the oven to 400°F (200°C).
2. In a large bowl, combine the flour and salt and make a well in the center.
3. Add the water and stir until a smooth dough is obtained.
4. Cover and set aside.
5. In a bowl, combine the lemon juice and zest, herbs, garlic and oil. Season to taste. Reserve.
6. Divide the dough into four portions and roll out four squares large enough to cover each grouse.
7. Place one grouse in the center of each square of dough.
8. Brush the birds with the lemon mixture and place the rest in the cavity.
9. Close the dough and pinch to seal, moistening the edges. Let stand for 5 minutes.
10. Bake on a greased baking sheet until the crust is golden, about 45 minutes.
11. Remove from the oven and let stand for 15 minutes before serving.

Chukar

The Chukar *(Alectoris chukar)*, a native of India, is also known as the Barbary chukar, Chuk, Indian chukar, Red-leg, and Rock Partridge. The chukar exists in several subspecies that range from the eastern Mediterranean to Northern India and China. Cock birds are kept as fighting stock in parts of Central Asia. It is a close relative of several varieties of Red-legged Partridges found across Europe.

Chukar partridges were introduced into the United States from Europe as game birds as early as 1893 – 800,000 were released in 1932 alone – and have naturalized in mountainous semi-desert areas of Northern California, Nevada, and Oregon. The Chukar lives on rocky, mountain slopes, or canyon walls. Steep, brush-covered slopes are their preferred cover, resulting in strenuous and exciting hunts. Chukars are also found in desert regions and on barren plateaus. The birds usually feed and roost in coveys of about 20 individuals. The chukar diet consists of weed seeds, grasses, berries, and the bulbs, leaves, and buds of various plants.

Chukars are marked by a black band running across the forehead, through the eyes, and down the neck. The lower breast and back are generally gray. The Chukar runs uphill to escape danger and will fly downhill. The birds are tame and easily raised in captivity and are a mainstay of hunting preserves and hunting reserves throughout the United States.

Young birds under the age of eight months, both male and female, have tender, delectable meat and cook much more quickly than adult birds. Both, however, must be barded or at least basted with fat or cooking juices to prevent them from drying out while cooking. Chukar can be:

- roasted (Lebanese-Style Marinated Chukar);
- braised (no recipe in this section);
- grilled (Grilled Chukar with Blackberries);
- simmered (Chukar Chowder with Pesto).

Since the chukar and the gray partridge are quite similar, they can be used interchangeably in the recipes. Chukar is particularly delicious when cooked with berries (Roast Chukar with Juniper Berries); citrus fruit (Grilled Chukar with Citrus Fruits and Herbs). Some cooks like to prepare chukar with roast pork.

* Bard (to): To tie fat around lean meats or fowl to keep them from drying out during roasting. The fat bastes the meat while it cooks (keeping it moist and adding flavor).

Chukar Chowder
with Pesto

*To make a more substantial dish,
uncooked cubed potatoes or rice may
be added 15 minutes before the end.*

Ingredients

2 tbsp	butter **or** oil	**30 ml**
1	onion, chopped	**1**
2	cloves garlic, crushed	**2**
1	stalk celery, sliced	**1**
3 cups	poultry stock	**750 ml**
1/4 cup	white wine	**60 ml**
1/2 cup	tomato sauce	**125 ml**
2	whole chukars	**2**
	salt and freshly ground pepper to taste	
2-3 tbsp	pesto	**30-45 ml**
1/2 cup	green beans, cut into pieces	**125 ml**
1/3 cup	15% light cream	**80 ml**

Garnish:

fresh basil

Method

1. Heat the butter in a saucepan and cook the onion, garlic and celery over medium heat for 3 to 4 minutes.
2. Add the stock, wine and tomato sauce and bring to a boil.
3. Place the chukars in the hot liquid and cook for 20 to 25 minutes, or until the meat separates easily from the bone.
4. While the chukars cook, add salt and pepper and half of the pesto.
5. Remove the chukars from the stock. Debone and dice the meat.
6. Return the meat to the stock and add the green beans. Simmer for 2 to 3 minutes.
7. Add the cream. Adjust the seasoning and add the remaining pesto.
8. Sprinkle with basil and serve immediately.

Roast Chukar with Juniper Berries

Ingredients

2	chukars	2
1 cup	poultry stock	250 ml
1	shallot, finely chopped	1
1 tbsp	butter	15 ml
1/2 cup	sherry **or** port	125 ml
1 tbsp	butter	15 ml
1 tbsp	flour	15 ml
7-10	whole juniper berries	7-10
	salt and freshly ground pepper to taste	
	sugar to taste	

Method

1. Preheat the oven to 350°F (180°C).
2. Roast the chukars for 30 to 35 minutes, basting frequently with the stock.
3. Pour off the cooking juices. Turn the oven off and leave the birds in the oven.
4. To make the sauce, cook the shallot in the butter and deglaze with the sherry or port. Reduce by half.
5. Add the cooking juices and bring to a boil.
6. Mix the butter and flour to obtain a paste. Whisk the mixture into the liquid. Add the juniper berries. Simmer for 5 minutes. Adjust the seasoning and add sugar if necessary.
7. Serve the chukars with the sauce.

Grilled Chukar
with Citrus Fruit and Herbs

The birds should be cooked slowly so that the herbs and zests can release their flavors. Lower the grill temperature if necessary.

Ingredients

2	chukars	2
1	bouquet of herbs, washed and dried (tarragon, oregano, basil, coriander, savory, etc.)	1
2	citrus fruits (orange, lemon or lime)	2
	salt and freshly ground pepper to taste	

Method

1. Preheat the barbecue to medium-hot.
2. Pack the herbs and citrus zests between the skin and the meat of the chukars.
3. Squeeze the juice from the fruit and use to baste the chukars while they cook.
4. Season generously on all sides.
5. Cook at medium-low heat on the grill or on a spit for 45 to 50 minutes, basting frequently.
6. Cut the chukars in half and serve with grilled vegetables.

Grilled Chukar
with Blackberries

Ingredients

Stuffing:

1/2 lb	uncooked ground poultry meat	225 g
1	shallot, chopped	1
1/3 cup	fresh or thawed blackberries	80 ml
2 tsp	chopped herbs (basil, tarragon, rosemary, thyme, etc.)	10 ml
	freshly ground pepper to taste	
2	whole chukars	2

Sauce:

1 tbsp	butter	15 ml
1	shallot, chopped	1
1 tbsp	flour	15 ml
1/4 cup	red wine	60 ml
3/4 cup	brown poultry stock	180 ml
1/4 cup	fresh or thawed blackberries	60 ml
	salt and freshly ground pepper to taste	
	chopped fresh herbs (basil, tarragon, rosemary, thyme, etc.)	

Method

1. Combine the stuffing ingredients. Stuff the cavity of the birds, without applying too much pressure, and tie to close.

2. Place the chukars on a sheet of oiled aluminum foil and brown on a preheated grill over high heat. Lower the heat to medium and cook for 30 to 35 minutes.

3. In the meantime, melt the butter in a skillet and sauté the shallot.

4. Sprinkle with the flour and stir to obtain a roux, letting the flour brown lightly.

5. Deglaze with the red wine and whisk in the stock.

6. Carefully add the blackberries and simmer until the sauce thickens.

7. Season and add the fresh herbs at the last minute.

8. Cut the chukars in half and serve with the sauce. Garnish with fresh blackberries and a few sprigs of herbs.

Lebanese-Style
Marinated Chukar

Ingredients

Marinade:

	juice of 2 lemons	
1/2 cup	olive oil	125 ml
4	cloves garlic, chopped	4
1 tsp	ground hot pepper	5 ml
2 tsp	ground cumin	10 ml
2 tsp	dried thyme	10 ml
1 tsp	cinnamon	5 ml
	freshly ground pepper to taste	

2	chukars, cut in half	2
	salt to taste	

Garlic Sauce:

3/4 cup	yogurt	180 ml
1-2	cloves garlic, chopped	1-2
1-2 tbsp	chopped fresh mint	15-30 ml
	salt and freshly ground pepper to taste	

Method

1. Combine all the marinade ingredients.
2. Marinate the chukar halves for 30 minutes to 6 hours.
3. Drain well and cook on the grill or in an oven preheated to 400°F (200°C) for 25 to 30 minutes. Salt the meat while it cooks.
4. Serve with pita bread, lettuce, sliced tomatoes, garlic sauce or hummus.

Garlic Sauce

1. Combine all the ingredients at least 30 minutes before serving.

Hungarian Partridge

When startled, a covey of Hungarian Partridge will rise in a group with a whir of flailing wings and squealing chirps. The birds generally fly in a straight line, but will often wheel together before scattering to land after a short distance. They are observant and wary and will travel rapidly on the ground, making for a challenging and occasionally frustrating hunt.

The Hungarian, or Gray partridge, *(Perdix perdix)* is a native of Europe and the Hungarian partridge population in Washington, Oregon, Idaho, Montana, and the Dakotas is possibly descended from birds released in Canada. The Hungarian has adapted well to the climate of Alberta and Saskatchewan and is most commonly found in open farmland and brush. Hungarian partridges are slightly larger than a Bobwhite quail and have a gray breast with chestnut-colored markings on the upper abdomen.

The back is mottled brown, gray, and white with dark brown wings and chestnut tail. Coveys of Hungarians, generally averaging 14 or more birds, will often remain in one location for many years.

Hungarian partridge has a delicate flavor that is less refined than that of quail or pheasant. Since partridge has a strong taste, it combines well with strongly flavored ingredients for example: roasted with ginger and lemon, or stuffed with cranberries and rosemary. Hungarian partridge can be:

- grilled (no recipe in this section);
- simmered (Mexican-Style Partridge Soup);
- roasted (Hungarian Partridge with Ginger and lemon);
- braised (Simple Paella).

Serve with distinctively-flavored side dishes.

Mexican-Style Partridge Soup

Ingredients

2 tsp	oil	10 ml
1	onion, chopped	1
1	clove garlic, crushed	1
4 cups	stock	1 l
2	Hungarian partridges	2
	salt to taste	
1/2 cup	frozen corn kernels	125 ml
2	Italian tomatoes, peeled and diced	2
	hot pepper sauce to taste	
2	ripe avocados, diced	2
1/4 cup	chopped fresh coriander	60 ml
1	lime, quartered	1

Method

1. In a large pot, heat the oil over medium heat and cook the onion and garlic for 4 to 5 minutes.

2. Add the stock and the partridges. Bring to a boil and simmer for 30 to 40 minutes. Salt to taste.

3. Remove the partridges from the stock. Debone and dice the meat. In the meantime, add the corn to the stock and cook for 2 minutes.

4. Add the partridge pieces, diced tomatoes and pepper sauce and bring to a boil.

5. Just before serving, garnish with the diced avocados and the coriander.

6. Serve immediately, accompanied with a lime quarter and nachos.

Hungarian Partridge
with Cranberry-Rosemary Stuffing

Ingredients

Stuffing:

1/2 lb	uncooked ground poultry meat	225 g
1	clove garlic	1
1	shallot, chopped	1
1/2 cup	chopped fresh or frozen cranberries	125 ml
1/4 cup	toasted pine nuts	60 ml
1 tbsp	lemon zest	15 ml
2 tsp	chopped fresh rosemary	10 ml
	salt and freshly ground pepper to taste	
2	Hungarian partridges, cut in half	2

Cranberry-Lemon Sauce:

1 tbsp	butter	15 ml
1	shallot, chopped	1
1 tbsp	flour	15 ml
1/3 cup	white wine	80 ml
2 cups	poultry stock	500 ml
1 tsp	lemon zest	5 ml
1	sprig fresh rosemary	1
1/3 cup	chopped fresh or frozen cranberries	80 ml
	pinch of sugar, if needed	
	salt and freshly ground pepper to taste	

Method

1. Preheat the oven to 350°F (180°C).
2. Combine all the stuffing ingredients and fill the cavity of the partridges, without applying too much pressure.
3. Place the partridges in an ovenproof dish. Truss, if necessary.
4. Bake in the center of the oven for 45 minutes to 1 hour.
5. In the meantime, prepare the sauce. In a saucepan, melt the butter and sauté the shallot.
6. Sprinkle with the flour and blend well to make a roux.
7. Deglaze with the wine and whisk in the stock.
8. Add the lemon zest, rosemary and cranberries and simmer until the sauce has thickened.
9. Sweeten if necessary and season to taste. Remove the rosemary.
10. Arrange the stuffed partridges on individual plates and top with the sauce.

Hungarian Partridge
with Ginger and Lemon

Ingredients

3 tbsp	toasted sesame oil	45 ml
2 tbsp	ginger	30 ml
2	Hungarian partridges, cut in half	2
1/2	onion, sliced	1/2
1/2 cup	quartered mushrooms	125 ml
1	red pepper, sliced	1
1/2 cup	lemon juice and zest	125 ml
1 tbsp	sugar	15 ml
1/2 cup	poultry stock	125 ml
1 tbsp	cornstarch	15 ml
1 tbsp	cold water	15 ml
	salt and freshly ground pepper to taste	
1	green onion, thinly sliced	1
1 tbsp	sesame seeds	15 ml

Method

1. Preheat the oven to 400°F (200°C).
2. Combine the oil and ginger and brush onto the partridges.
3. Bake in the center of the oven for 30 to 35 minutes.
4. In the meantime, heat the remaining oil mixture in a saucepan and cook the vegetables over low heat.
5. Add the lemon juice and zest, sugar and stock.
6. Bring to a boil and thicken the sauce with the cornstarch that has been dissolved in the cold water. Cook until thickened. Season to taste.
7. Serve the partridges with the sauce and garnish with the green onion and sesame seeds.

Simple Paella

Ingredients

2	Hungarian partridges, cut into quarters	2
2 tbsp	oil	30 ml
1	onion, chopped	1
1	red pepper, julienned	1
1	green pepper, julienned	1
2	cloves garlic, chopped	2
1 cup	thickly sliced green onions	250 ml
1 cup	fresh or frozen green peas	250 ml
12	mussels	12
2 cups	long-grain rice	500 ml
12	shrimp, uncooked	12
6	tomatoes, crushed	6
2	pinches of saffron	2
	ground cayenne pepper to taste	
	salt and freshly ground pepper to taste	

Method

1. In a large skillet, sauté the partridge pieces in the oil.
2. Add the vegetables and continue cooking for a few more minutes.
3. In a large pot, bring salted water to a boil and add the mussels until the shells open. Remove the mussels.
4. Soak the rice in the mussel water, about 4 to 5 minutes.
5. Add the vegetables, partridge pieces, shrimp and tomatoes.
6. Add the saffron and cayenne and season with the salt and pepper.
7. Cover and bake in the oven at 350°F (180°C) for 25 to 30 minutes. Five to 10 minutes before the end, place the mussels on the paella. Let stand for 10 minutes before serving.

Mourning Dove

Throughout North America, large flocks of doves can be seen in the fall descending onto harvested wheat and cornfields to forage for waste grain amid the stubble. Well adapted to both rural and urban environments and a prolific breeder, the mourning dove is among the most important game bird species and early fall dove hunts are features of many communities across America.

The mourning dove, *(Zenaida macroura)*, is a migratory bird with a range that extends form southern Canada to as far south as Costa Rica and Panama. Most over-winter in the southeastern United States. Mourning doves have dull gray upper bodies with blackish wings and an underside that ranges from white near the throat to a buff breast and belly. Swift and far-ranging flyers, doves travel daily in pairs or loose-knit flocks between food and water sources. The birds roost in trees at night and many a nocturnal traveler has had the heart-stopping experience of starting a cedar or pine tree full of doves into an eruption of wing-whistling flight. Their preferred diet includes weed seeds and waste grains – particularly wheat and buckwheat.

In North America the order to which morning doves belong, the Columbiformes, are also represented by the white-winged dove, encountered in the southwestern United States and Mexico, and the prolific Rock dove or domestic pigeon, an imported species that has spread across the continent. Other relatives include the common ground dove of the Deep South and the tiny Inca dove of Mexico.

Traditionally young birds, known as squab, have been preferred for roasting. Squab can be easily recognized by their light-reddish breast meat and plump legs. Squab is available prepared and frozen from specialty food producers. Older birds are best served in a stew or casserole. Doves can be:

• roasted (Doves Stuffed with Sausage Meat);
• grilled (Dove Packets with Thyme and Mustard);
• braised (Doves Braised with Fennel);
• simmered (Pot au Feu with Artichokes).

When roasting small game birds like dove, be sure that your oven is thoroughly preheated, since they will require only a short cooking time under high heat.

Doves Braised with Fennel

Ingredients

2 tbsp	butter	30 ml
1	fennel bulb, thinly sliced	1
1	onion, thinly sliced	1
1	bay leaf	1
1	sprig fresh thyme	1
1 1/2 cups	brown poultry stock	375 ml
4	doves, skinned and cut into quarters	4
	salt and freshly ground pepper to taste	

Method

1. In a saucepan, melt the butter and cook the fennel and onion for 2 to 3 minutes.

2. Add the bay leaf, thyme sprig and stock. Bring to a boil.

3. Add the dove pieces and season with salt and pepper. Cover and simmer over low heat for 20 to 30 minutes, depending on the size of the pieces.

4. Correct the seasoning. Serve four pieces of dove per person on a bed of fennel.

Doves with Garlic and Herbs

To turn this recipe into a complete meal, add vegetables and potatoes before putting the dish in the oven.

Ingredients

5	cloves garlic, finely sliced	**5**
1	stalk celery, chopped	**1**
1	carrot, finely chopped	**1**
3 tbsp	oil	**45 ml**
4	doves, skinned and cut into quarters	**4**
	flour	
1/2 cup	white wine	**125 ml**
2 cups	brown poultry stock	**500 ml**
1/3 cup	chopped fresh herbs of your choice (thyme, basil, oregano)	**80 ml**
1	bay leaf	**1**
	salt and freshly ground pepper to taste	

Method

1. Preheat the oven to 375°F (190°C).

2. In a skillet, sauté the garlic, celery and carrot in 1 tbsp (15 ml) oil, over low heat, until nice and golden. Place in an ovenproof dish.

3. Dredge the dove pieces in flour. Shake off any excess.

4. In the same skillet, brown the dove pieces in the remaining oil.

5. Deglaze the skillet with the white wine and reduce by half.

6. Add the stock, herbs and bay leaf. Bring to a boil and pour the mixture into the ovenproof dish. Season, cover and bake in the center of the oven for 30 to 40 minutes.

Doves with Creamed Onions

Ingredients

3	Spanish onions, sliced	3
2 tbsp	butter	30 ml
1 1/2 cups	35% whipping cream	375 ml
1	bay leaf	1
1	sprig fresh thyme **or**	1
	pinch of dried thyme	
	salt and freshly ground pepper to taste	
4	doves, cut into quarters	4
1/4 cup	poultry stock	60 ml

Method

1. Preheat the oven to 400°F (200°C).

2. In an skillet dish, cook the onions in the butter over low heat until translucent.

3. Stir in the cream, bay leaf and thyme. Season to taste and continue cooking, uncovered, stirring often until the mixture is very thick.

4. Meanwhile, bake the dove pieces in the oven for 15 to 20 minutes, basting frequently with the poultry stock.

5. Place a generous portion of the onion mixture on each of the dove pieces and broil in the oven.

6. Serve four dove pieces per person, accompanied with mixed beans.

Grilled Doves with Red Wine and Tomato Sauce

Ingredients

1 tbsp	oil	15 ml
2	onions, chopped	2
2	cloves garlic, chopped	2
1/2 cup	red wine	125 ml
1 can (19 oz)	diced tomatoes	1 can (540 ml)
1	bay leaf	1
1 tbsp	dried basil	15 ml
2 tsp	dried oregano	10 ml
	salt and freshly ground pepper to taste	
4	doves, cut in half	4
1/4 cup	poultry stock	60 ml

Method

1. In a saucepan, heat the oil and cook the onions and garlic for 2 to 3 minutes.

2. Deglaze the saucepan with the red wine and reduce by a third.

3. Add the tomatoes, bay leaf, basil and oregano. Simmer over low heat for 15 to 20 minutes, or until the sauce has thickened. Season to taste.

4. Meanwhile, grill the dove halves over medium heat, basting frequently with the stock, for 10 to 15 minutes.

5. Serve the dove halves on a bed of the tomato sauce, accompanied with fresh pasta or polenta.

Pot-au-Feu with Artichokes

Ingredients

1 tbsp	oil	**15 ml**
1 tbsp	butter	**15 ml**
4	doves, cut into quarters	**4**
1	leek, cut into pieces	**1**
2	carrots, sliced	**2**
2	stalks celery, cut into pieces	**2**
3 cups	poultry stock	**750 ml**
12	small potatoes, quartered	**12**
1	bouquet garni	**1**
12	artichoke hearts, halved	**12**
	salt and freshly ground pepper to taste	

Method

1. In a pot, heat the oil and melt the butter. Brown the dove pieces on all sides.

2. Add the vegetables and cook for another 3 to 4 minutes.

3. Add the stock, potatoes and bouquet garni. Season to taste and simmer over low heat, covered, for 15 to 20 minutes.

4. Add the artichoke hearts and cook for another 10 minutes.

5. Adjust the seasoning and serve immediately.

Dove Gumbo

Ingredients

1 tbsp	oil	15 ml
1 tbsp	butter	15 ml
4	doves, cut into quarters	4
3 tbsp	flour seasoned with salt and pepper	45 ml
2	onions, sliced	2
2	cloves garlic, crushed	2
2	stalks celery, sliced	2
1 tbsp	chili powder	15 ml
1 can (19 oz)	diced tomatoes	1 can (540 ml)
3 tbsp	tomato paste	45 ml
1 1/4 cups	poultry stock	310 ml
1/2 cup	red wine	125 ml
1	red pepper, sliced	1
1	green pepper, sliced	1
24	small okra pods, fresh or frozen	24
3	corn cobs, cut into chunks	3
1 tbsp	lemon juice	15 ml
	pinch of sugar	
	salt and freshly ground pepper to taste	

Method

1. In a pot, heat the oil and melt the butter. Dredge the dove pieces in the seasoned flour and brown them in the pot. Remove and reserve.

2. In the same pot, cook the onion and garlic until translucent. Add the celery, chili powder and the remaining flour.

3. Stir in the tomatoes, tomato paste, stock, wine and dove pieces. Bring to a boil.

4. Add the vegetables, lemon juice and sugar. Cover and cook over medium heat for 30 to 35 minutes.

5. Adjust the seasoning and serve immediately.